TWO GUIDEPOSTS FOR INHERITING THE KINGDOM

WITHIN THE VEIL
&
OUTSIDE THE CAMP

Stephen Kaung

ISBN: 978-1-942521-51-8

Available from:

Christian Testimony Ministry
4424 Huguenot Road
Richmond, Virginia 23235

www.christiantestimonyministry.com

Printed in USA

CONTENTS

WITHIN THE VEIL

See that ye refuse not him that speaks. For if those did not escape who had refused him who uttered the oracles on earth, much more we who turn away from him who does so from heaven: whose voice then shook the earth; but now he has promised, saying, Yet once will I shake not only the earth, but also the heaven. But this Yet once, signifies the removing of what is shaken, as being made, that what is not shaken may remain. Wherefore let us, receiving a kingdom not to be shaken, have grace, by which let us serve God acceptably with reverence and fear. For also our God is a consuming fire. (Hebrews. 12:25-29)

Wherein God, willing to show more abundantly to the heirs of the promise the unchangeableness of his purpose, intervened by an oath, that by two unchangeable things, in which it was impossible that God should lie, we might have a strong encouragement, who have fled for refuge to lay hold on the hope set before us, which we have as an anchor of the soul, both secure and firm, and entering into that within the veil, where Jesus is entered as forerunner for us, become for ever a high priest according to the order of Melchisedec. (Hebrews 6:17-20)

Having therefore, brethren, boldness for entering into the holy of holies by the blood of Jesus, the new and living way which he has dedicated for us through the veil, that is, his flesh, and having a great priest over the house of God, let us approach with a true heart, in full assurance of faith, sprinkled as to our hearts from a wicked conscience, and washed as to our body with pure water. Let us hold fast the confession of the hope unwavering, (for he is faithful who has promised;) and let us consider one another for provoking to love and good works; not forsaking the assembling of ourselves together, as the custom is with some; but encouraging one another, and by so much the more as ye see the day drawing near. (Hebrews 10:19-25)

This letter to the Hebrews was written to Hebrews who turned to be Christians in the first century. The Spirit of God gave this letter to prepare them for the coming catastrophe—God was going to shake not only the earth but also heaven. In other words, God is not only going to shake earthly things, secular things, but He is going to shake heavenly or so-called spiritual things.

God was going to do such a shaking at that time because He wanted to shake loose those Hebrews who became Christians from the bondage of Judaism into the liberty of Christ. By the destruction of Jerusalem and the destruction of the holy temple in Jerusalem, the Hebrews who became Christians in the first century were finally broken loose from Moses into Christ.

We believe this book is very relevant for us today. It is not only relevant, but it is urgent. Why? because we are living in a time that God is shaking not only the earth but also the heaven. Christianity has become so Judaized that God wants to shake His people out of Christianity into Christ.

Christianity is like a shadow that should introduce us to the substance that is Christ; but instead of that, Christianity today has become a substitute for Christ and God is very jealous for

His Son. God will not allow anything to compare or to compete with His Son. That is why today we find everything around us is being shaken. We find that not only the whole world is in a great shaking but the Christian world is also in great shaking. Even in our personal spiritual experience we are under great shaking. Why? Because it is the will of God that that which can be removed shall be removed. Only that which cannot be removed shall remain, because it is God's will for us to inherit the kingdom that cannot be shaken.

During this time of great shaking, how will God keep His people from being shaken away and keep them pure and blameless until the day of Christ? You notice that in this book of Hebrews there are two phrases which are very catching: "within the veil" and "outside the camp." These two phrases are guideposts for God's people that they may be kept through the great shaking and inherit the kingdom that cannot be shaken. For this time, we would like to just focus our attention on this matter—within the veil.

I think probably a little history is needed. After God redeemed His children of Israel and delivered them out of Egypt, He took them through the Red Sea to the foot of Mount Sinai. There God gave them the ten commandments—the law. Actually, the giving of the law was not the purpose of God concerning His people; the giving of the law was just a preparation or an introduction. The purpose of God with His people was revealed by God commanding Moses to build Him a tabernacle.

GOD'S PURPOSE SHOWN IN THE TABERNACLE

We must remember that it is not God's purpose to put us under the law that we may be condemned. It is God's purpose that He may dwell among His people. In order that He could dwell among His people, He had to give them the commandments to let them know themselves so that they would appreciate Him and His grace. Hence, the purpose of God is shown in the tabernacle. God told Moses, "Build Me a sanctuary, a tabernacle that I may dwell among My people." We know that this is God's eternal thought. Even before He created man, God had this thought in Him—He wanted to dwell among man. How was He to dwell among man? How was He to dwell among the children of Israel whom He had just delivered out of Egypt? By a tabernacle.

If you know something about the tabernacle, you know that outside the tabernacle was the court. All the children of Israel could enter into this court and bring their sacrifices to God and the priests would sacrifice these on the brazen altar.

Within the outer court there was the holy place—the place where the priests could enter. The children of Israel could not enter into the holy place, only the priests—those whom God had set apart for His service. There they would light the golden lampstand, they would put the shewbread on the table of shewbread, and they would burn incense on the golden altar of incense.

Behind the holy place was the holiest of all. The holiest of all was where the presence of God dwelt. Here was the ark of the covenant and above the ark, as the cover of the ark, the mercy seat. God's glory dwelt on the mercy seat between the two cherubim.

Between the holy place and the holiest of all was a veil, a very heavy veil. We are told that even if you put two oxen or two horses on opposite sides and tried to pull the veil, you could not break it. It was a very heavy veil, and it separated the holy place and the holiest of all.

No one could enter into the holiest of all. The children of Israel could not enter into the holiest of all, nor could the priests; only the high priest. Once a year, on the Day of Atonement, he would enter behind the veil with blood and the smoke of incense to cover him. There he would make atonement for himself and for the nation of Israel, and after he did that he quickly retreated.

You will find God wanted to dwell among His people; God wanted to have fellowship with His people. Yet, even though this was the desire of the Lord, it seems as if God were saying, "You cannot have fellowship with Me." On the one hand, God called them to come to Him; yet on the other hand, He said, "Stay away because I am holy."

Now these things being thus ordered, into the first tabernacle the priests enter at all times, accomplishing the services; but into the second, the high priest only, once a year, not without blood, which he offers for himself and for the errors of the people: the Holy Spirit shewing this, that the way of the holy of holies has not yet been made manifest while as yet the first tabernacle has its standing; the which is an image for the present time, according to which both gifts and sacrifices, unable to perfect as to conscience him that worshipped, are offered, consisting only of meats and drinks and divers washings, ordinances of flesh, imposed until the time of setting things right. But Christ being come . . . (Hebrews 9:6-11a)

Here you find the tabernacle by which God dwelt among His people. Even though the people could come to the court to offer sacrifices, even though the priests could enter into the holy place to serve God, and yet the way to the holy of holies had not been opened. The very fact that the high priest could only go in once a year proved that the way to the holy of holies had not yet been opened. In other words, all these sacrifices, all these ordinances were but shadow. They were there serving as a type, a shadow and they were there until the time of setting things right. The time of setting things right is the time when Christ is come.

In Exodus 26, you find how the veil that was to be put between the holy place and the holiest of all was made. It was made of blue, of purple, of scarlet, of twined linen, and embroidered all over with artistic work of cherubim. This veil was to separate the holiest of all from the holy place and from the court.

THE EARTHLY LIFE OF OUR LORD JESUS

In Hebrews 10, we find that our Lord Jesus has opened a new and living way for us through the veil, that is His flesh. So the veil in the tabernacle is a type of the flesh of our Lord Jesus; that is to say, this veil represents the earthly life of our Lord Jesus. The Word became flesh and tabernacled among men, full of grace and truth.

When our Lord Jesus became man upon this earth, His flesh is represented by the veil that separated the holiest of all from the holy place. What does that mean? Blue is the color of heaven. Purple is the color of wealth, because in the old days the wealthy people were dressed in purple. Scarlet is the color of royalty. Linen, in the Scripture, represents purity. So you find that the life of our Lord Jesus on earth was heavenly, was rich, was royal, and was pure.

Can you ever find a life on earth so pure as the life of our Lord Jesus? He is like the fine linen. Everything about Him is pure; not only clean, but pure. You know, there is a difference between cleanness and pureness. Clean is without any defilement, but pure is singleness. The life of our Lord Jesus is such a pure life. His life is pure towards God. There is no ulterior motive in Him. His whole life is governed by the Father's will—a life that is clean and pure. No one could point out any sin in Him. He challenged people and said, "Can you point out any sin in Me?" He is the sinless One. He has never committed any sin. He does not know what sin is; but He is more than that—He is pure. He always obeyed His Father.

His life on earth is like the twined linen, and you find it is mixed with blue—heavenly. Even though He walked on earth, He is in heaven. He said, "No one has ever ascended to heaven but He who has descended from heaven." He is yet in heaven. So our Lord Jesus, while He was on earth, was a heavenly man. Wherever He goes He brings with Him a heavenly atmosphere. His touch is a heavenly touch. He is different. He is in the world but He is not of the world because He belongs to heaven.

There you will find the riches of Him. Even though He was born in a manger, even though He was born and reared in a carpenter's family, yet He is so rich—the riches of His grace, the riches of truth in Him.

Then of course, He is so royal—scarlet. Though He is humble, yet He is so majestic; He is so royal. You can see the kingly manner in Him. He was in control over every situation. That was the life of our Lord Jesus. There was never a human life on earth like that of the Lord Jesus.

There on the veil were the cherubim embroidered all over. Cherubim, so far as I understand it, represent the divine, original concept of God toward creation. In other words, before God created all things He had an original concept about them—the pattern. He had an idea what creation should be, what the created being should be, and these are represented by the cherubim. So, we find that the cherubim were embroidered all over that veil. In other words, the life of our Lord Jesus answered completely to God's concept of what creation should be. He was *the* man, the man after God's own heart, the man that God created for Himself. Adam, the first man that was created, failed; and when he sinned he was driven out from the garden of Eden, and God set up cherubim to guard the way to the tree of life. In other words, God said, "Now you have fallen, but My divine concept will never change. It still remains and I will get what I am going to get."

God got His man in Christ Jesus. This is the man. He was the veil. The veil had two sides. The inner side of the veil faced the mercy seat. So far as the Lord, Himself, was concerned, He lived such a life on earth that He was in constant communion with His Father. He saw His Father's face all the time. He pleased His Father all the time and His Father said, "This is My beloved Son in whom I am well-pleased. I am happy with Him."

On the other hand, this veil separated everything outside the veil from the holiest of all. Only the Lord Jesus, as the man after God's own heart, had the right and the privilege to dwell in God's presence. He was the only one who was worthy. He was the only one who could dwell in God's presence. Nobody else could because if anybody else dared to enter within the veil without the blood, he would be smitten to death. God is holy. No one who is not holy can see God, and that is why no one could enter behind the veil. Who could stand before the holy God? Who could live in the presence of God? Nobody could. Therefore, the strange thing was, the life of our Lord Jesus was so perfect that He was the only one who could live in the presence of God; but at the same time, He became the veil that separated us from God's presence.

Some people say we need to imitate Christ. Some people say Christ came into the world to set an example for us and we should copy Him, follow Him. But do you know that the very life of Christ on earth, instead of saving us, actually condemns us? If Christ had not come, you would not have a perfect example of the life that pleases God; you would have nothing with which to compare. But with the coming of Christ, you have a perfect example of the man of God's heart. Will not His life condemn you instead of save you? The more you see the life of the Lord Jesus the more you are condemned, because He is worthy but you are not. He can see the Father's face but you cannot. His life will condemn you.

THE VEIL WAS RENT

He is the veil, but thank God that veil was rent. The Lord Jesus came into this world not just to exhibit the perfect life. The Lord Jesus came to this earth in order to die. He was the Perfect man, the One who was sinless, but He was made sin for us that we might become the righteousness of God. It is not the life of our Lord Jesus on earth that saves us; it is the death of our Lord Jesus on the cross that saves us.

Our Lord Jesus came into this world. He bore His cross all His life; the shadow of the cross cast over His whole life. Then finally He was brought outside the city of Jerusalem to Golgotha, and there He was crucified. A marvelous thing happened. When Christ cried out with a loud voice, "It is finished," and gave up His Spirit to the Father in Golgotha, outside the city of Jerusalem, at that very moment, the heavy veil in the temple of Jerusalem was rent in two from top to bottom (See Mt. 27). This veil that separated the holiest from the holy place was rent at the very moment when Christ died. It was rent from top to bottom, not from bottom to top. In other words, it was not rent by human hands. God rent the veil. On Calvary's cross, God broke the body of Christ, and there in the temple, God rent the veil. When the veil was rent, what happened? The way to the holiest was opened.

How we do praise and thank God that today the veil is rent! That which separates us from God is now removed. Christ has opened a new and living way for us into the holiest of all. Do you know that before Christ died no one could live in God's presence? But today, because Christ has died, the veil has been rent. There is no reason for you not to live in God's presence. A life within the veil is the right and the privilege of every believer today. Are you living there? In the past, such a life was impossible, but now such a life is your portion. Why not live within the veil?

Many Christians today are still living in the outer court. Some Christians are living in the holy place. But remember, Christ has opened a new and living way for us to live in the very presence of God in the holiest of all. This is our portion.

In the outer court, people came to offer sacrifices. We may say as believers that we do preach the Gospel, we do help people and point people to Christ. It is like offering sacrifices on the brazen altar. This is our relationship with the world, but this is not the place where we live.

In the holy place, the priests serve. Now it is true, as the priests of God we not only serve the world by preaching the Gospel, helping people, pointing people to Christ, but we also serve God. In what sense? By lighting the lampstand. That is to say, we bear the testimony of Jesus. The Church is like the lampstand that bears the light and the light is Christ. So we bear the testimony of Jesus with our life and we tell people with our words who Jesus is, what He is to us. This is our testimony. We also exhibit Christ, which is like putting the shewbread on the table of shewbread. At the Lord's table, when we break the bread and drink the cup, we exhibit the death of Christ; we exhibit Him. We also burn the incense in the sense that we pray and worship. That is true.

WHERE DO WE LIVE?

In the outer court, to the world, we preach the Gospel. In the holy place, in the church, we serve and worship God. But where do we live? We do not live in the outer court, nor do we live in the holy place. We should live in the holiest of all. If we live in the holiest of all, then we can serve God in His church and we can serve the world with the Gospel. Otherwise, how do we have the power for it? So the question is: Where do we live?

Do not think that to live a life within the veil is for a chosen few. If you know mysticism, the mystics will tell you this is a life for a chosen few only. If you are not among the chosen few, then this is not a life for you. But that is mysticism; that is not the Bible. The Word tells us that this life within the veil is the right of every believer, every child of God. We do not need to live in the outer court, far away from God, engaging in all kinds of activities but that's about all. Is our Christian life just activities? Very busy? Well, we should be busy, but is that all Christian life is? No. Or is it that our life is just that when we come together we worship, we exhibit? Is that all? No. God's purpose is that we may dwell in His very presence, that we may see His face day by day, that we may behold His glory. It is the life within the veil that Christ has provided for us.

How can we go through this time of shaking, when everything is being shaken around us? How can we go through this time if all our Christian life is just activities in the outer court? One day we may not be allowed to be active anymore. Then what will happen to us? If our

Christian life is only coming together to worship God, to exhibit Christ (thank God for that; we should do that), then what will happen when we are not allowed to meet? Will our Christian life collapse? Wreck? In many places in the world, Christians have found this out—their outward activities cannot save them; even the so-called church-life cannot save them.

Now I do not mean that we should not be active; we should. I do not mean that we should not have church-life; we should. But there is one thing that is basic; there is something foundational: We must have a life within the veil, because all these things, one day, will be shaken away. But thank God this life is ours. The veil is rent.

Many Christians today still seem to live before the veil, as if the veil has not been rent, as if the veil is still upon their face. They cannot see God. But brothers and sisters, remember this: The veil is rent. Christ has opened that new and living way for us and let us enter in.

THE LIFE WITHIN THE VEIL

Now what is meant by the life within the veil? Of course, in the Scriptures you find there are many different ways to describe this life within the veil. Remember, what is described is not for a select few. What is described actually is our common portion, our inheritance in Christ.

A HIDDEN LIFE

First of all, a life within the veil is a life hidden with Christ in God. In Colossians 3:3-4 it says that our life is hidden with Christ in God and Christ is our life. Do we have a hidden life? Is our life just a life before man? In other words, is our life just a life in the outer court? In the outer court people are there; in the outer court you are seen; in the outer court you are busily engaged, maybe helping people to bind the sacrifice and do all kinds of things. But do you have a life hidden with Christ in God? How much of that hidden life do you have?

Look at David. Before David was manifested to the nation of Israel, he had a hidden life unknown to man—not even his family knew about it—but known to God. While he was a shepherd tending the sheep, a lion came, a bear came. Under the anointing of God, how he broke the lion and the bear and delivered the sheep. This was something that happened to him, but was never broadcast; he had a hidden life with God. His life was hid with Christ in God.

How much of a hidden life do we have? Is our Christian life just a life before man? Of course, there must be a life before man because that is our testimony. But do you have a hidden life with God? In your daily life, is your life hid with Christ in God? Is there something going on between you and God unknown to man but known to God? This is a life within the veil. That kind of life will become your power, the power of your testimony, and because it is a life hidden with Christ in God, therefore it is beyond the touch of the enemy.

The Bible says we are seated with Christ in the heavenlies. He has not only quickened us out of death, He has not only raised us up from the dead together with Christ, but He has seated us with Christ in the heavenlies. That is to say, everything is under our feet. This is that life hidden with Christ in God. Do we have such a life? Remember, this is our right; Christ has opened it for us.

MAKING GOD OUR HOME

A life within the veil is a life that makes God our home. In Psalm 90, Moses said, "Thou art our dwelling place, O God; Thou art our dwelling place from generation to generation, in all generations." *Dwelling place* means "home." In other words, Moses realized that God is his home. A life within the veil is a life at home with God. Do you take God as your home?

The Scripture says, "God is my refuge." Thank God for the refuge, but He is more than a refuge. You flee to a refuge when you are in trouble, but you go home because that is your home. Many Christians take God as their refuge. Thank God for that. He is our refuge. When you are in trouble, cry to Him and He will answer you and He will deliver you. Thank God for that; but that is not good enough. God is your home. That is where you dwell—your dwelling place—that is where you live.

A Place of Rest

Home is a place of rest. Therefore, in Hebrews you will find we have a rest that is promised to us, and this rest is none other than a life behind the veil. We rest in God. We rest from our own works. It is not a place of striving and struggling, but it is a place that we rest by faith in Christ Jesus.

A Place of Love

Home is a place of love. We enjoy the love of God and we love God.

A Place of Satisfaction

Home is a place of satisfaction. We find satisfaction in God and God finds His satisfaction in us. I like the word in Habakkuk. Even though everything around him was not right, yet he said, "God is my delight; I am satisfied in God."

No matter how unsatisfying your environment may be, if you live a life behind the veil, you are satisfied in God. Make God your home. Stay there.

AN ABIDING LIFE

A life within the veil is a life of abiding. In John 15, the Lord said: "I am the true vine and ye are the branches. Abide in Me and I abide in you and you will bear much fruit."

He is the true vine and you are the branch, and you have a responsibility—abide in Him. Make your home in Him. Be in communication with Him. Do not let your communication with Him be interrupted by anything. If there is any sin—confess it. If there is any disobedience—surrender. Let there be nothing standing, interrupting your communion with Him.

It is a picture of union and communion. You will find the picture of the vine and the branches is one of union because the Lord said: "I am the vine, you are the branches." That is union. He does not say, "I am the root of the vine and ye are the branches." He says, "I am the vine." "I am the whole vine and ye are the branches; ye are part of Me." That is union and because there is union there ought to be communion. The sap of the vine will flow into every branch and if there is no interruption, then naturally all the

24

branches will bear much fruit. This is the life within the veil. There is union and communion and out of that union and communion there is fruitfulness.

What is fruit? There is a difference between fruit and work. Work is something that you do, you put on with effort. Fruit is something that is produced out of the abundance, out of the maturity of life. That is fruit. In a sense it is effortless, unconscious, but to the glory of God. It is a life of abiding. You live in Him, abide in Him.

A LIFE OF LIGHT

The life behind the veil is the life that is described by the apostle John in his first epistle. He says, "God is light; walk in the light as He is in the light and you have fellowship one with another and the blood of Jesus Christ, God's Son, cleanses you from all your sins."

God is light and you walk in the light. The light here is not artificial light. In the outer court you have the sunshine—created light. In the holy place, you have the light of the lampstand— artificial light. But in the holiest of all, you have the glory of God as light. In other words, God is light. If we live a life within the veil, then God is light. He shines in you and you walk in that light of life and you have fellowship with one another. If there is anything wrong, the blood of Jesus Christ cleanses you from all sin. It is a life walking in the light of God.

A LIFE OF PRACTICAL RIGHTEOUSNESS

It is a life of righteousness, practical righteousness. God is righteous. Therefore, he that is born of God must practice righteousness, practical righteousness in his daily life. We have to be right, and how can we be right? (Not that we can, but He who is our life can.) If we let Him live in us, then we will find that we will practice righteousness as He is righteous.

A LIFE OF LOVE

God is love. Therefore, let us love one another. Walk in love. How can you do that? If you live behind the veil, if you live before God, if you live by the life of Christ, then of course, His love in you will love out from you and you will be able to love the brethren, love the unlovely. It is a life behind the veil.

THE LAW OF THE SPIRIT OF LIFE

What is this life behind the veil? Romans 8 says the law of the Spirit of life set us free from the law of sin and death. When you are behind the veil, you will find the law of the Spirit of life functions. There, the law of the Spirit of life operates and when the Spirit of life operates, it overcomes the law of sin and death. The law of sin is: You do what you should not do; that is the law of sin. The law of death is: You cannot do what you should do; that is the law of death. Isn't it true that often we feel we cannot do what we should do and we do what we should not do? We are under the law of sin and of death. But thank God, if we live a life behind the veil, another law operates, a higher life operates—the law of the Spirit of life. In other words, life operates and this life is resurrection life. It overcomes even death. It is a victorious life. It is a glorious life.

A TRANSFORMING LIFE

Behind the veil, with unveiled face, you behold the glory of God face to face. There you will be transformed from glory to glory according to His image by the Lord, the Spirit. It is a transforming life.

If you want to be transformed according to His image, you have to live a life behind the veil, because if you live before the veil, you will not see His face. If you do not see Him, the Holy Spirit is not able to do the work of transformation. You have to see Him. Then He will put the desire within your heart to be like Him and the Holy Spirit will transform you from glory to glory according to His image.

So, this is the only life that we must live. Do not think we have some other kind of life we can choose to live. The Lord Jesus, through His death, the breaking of His body, has opened this new and living way for us. What a price He has paid for us that we may, by Him, live behind the veil, in the very presence of God, beholding His glory day by day, and be transformed! What a redemption He has accomplished for us! What he has done for us! Then He has said to come in and live within the veil. This is the only life for you. There is no other life.

Do not be contented to live in the outer court. You may live in the outer court for a long time; but the shaking is coming, and if that is the place where you live, you will be shaken off. Do not even live just in the holy place. It is good, but the shaking is coming. Even that is not enough. The only life that we must live is the life that Christ has ordained through His suffering for us. It is a life within the veil.

Oh, if only we can see that this is the life that Christ has opened for us and this is the only life that we must live; then we will not linger in the outer court nor even stay long in the holy place, but we will live in the holiest of all. Yes, we will come out and serve in the holy place and serve in the outer court, but we will live in the holiest of all—behind the veil.

In the book of Hebrews, we are told that the secret of passing through great shaking and remaining unshaken is to live behind the veil, within the veil. That is the secret and this is an open secret. It is open to everyone. So, may the Lord help us.

Shall we pray:

Dear heavenly Father, we do praise and thank Thee for the glorious redemption that our Lord Jesus has accomplished for us. Oh, how we praise and thank Thee that not only Thou has opened heaven to us, but Thou has even opened heaven to us today that we may daily live within the veil, beholding the glory of the Lord with unveiled face. And Father, we do thank Thee for this privilege and this right. This day we want to rise up and claim our right and take it as our own, because we know that this will honor Thee. This is the way You want us to live. So Lord, keep us there. We ask in the name of our Lord Jesus. Amen.

OUTSIDE THE CAMP

We have an altar of which they have no right to eat who serve the tabernacle; for of those beasts whose blood is carried as sacrifices for sin into the holy of holies by the high priest, of these the bodies are burned outside the camp. Wherefore also Jesus, that he might sanctify the people by his own blood, suffered without the gate: therefore let us go forth to him without the camp, bearing his reproach: for we have not here an abiding city, but we seek the coming one. By him therefore let us offer the sacrifice of praise continually to God, that is, the fruit of the lips confessing his name. But of doing good and communicating of your substance be not forgetful, for with such sacrifices God is well pleased. (Hebrews. 13:10-16)

The book of Hebrews was written to the Hebrew believers in the first century to prepare them for the shaking that was soon coming upon the world. We know that in AD 70, God allowed the city of Jerusalem and the temple in it to be completely destroyed. This was a great shaking to the Jewish people at that time. We cannot imagine what a great shaking it must have been to these people. This was a great shaking to the Hebrew believers too, because they tended to cling to Moses as they clung to Christ. But it was God's will that they should have been completely freed from the bondage of Judaism into the perfect liberty of Christ. God wanted these people to make a break from Moses into His Son, the Lord Jesus, and this shaking was to serve such purpose. Through the destruction of Jerusalem and its temple, the Hebrew believers were finally being released from Judaism into Christ, because this was the will of God.

This book of Hebrews is most relevant in our days because we are also in a time of great shaking. I think everybody can see that we live in the hour of shaking. Not only earthly things are being shaken, but also even heavenly or spiritual things are being shaken. The reason such shaking is taking place is that that which can be shaken will be removed so that that which cannot be shaken may remain. Anything that can be shaken shall be removed because God has given us a kingdom that cannot be shaken and He wants us to inherit that kingdom.

When such shaking is happening around the world, people are just frightened to death as they think of the things that are coming. But the Bible says this is the time that we who are the Lord's, who have been forewarned, foretold, should raise up our heads, for our redemption draws near.

Now, God prepared the Hebrew believers of the first century for this great shaking. He gave them definite instructions by which they could stand through the time of shaking and stand before God. We believe that the instructions given in this book are for us today.

There are two phrases in the book of Hebrews that serve as guideposts for us. One is: "within the veil"; that is, God wants us to live within the veil. This was a privilege that the people in the Old Testament time never had. Once a year, the high priest, by the blood and the smoke of the incense, entered into the holy of holies to make atonement for himself and for the people and he had to retreat very quickly. The

Holy Spirit indicated by this that the way to the holiest of all was not yet open. But thank God, through the death of our Lord Jesus, the veil that separated the holiest from the holy place was rent.

When our Lord Jesus died on the cross, at the very moment when He cried with a loud voice, "It is finished," and He gave up His spirit to the Father, there within the city in the temple that veil was rent from top to bottom. Because of the rent veil, the way to the holiest is open to us. We may enter in, and not only enter in but it is the will of God that we should dwell within. To live within the veil is now our privilege.

God does not want us just to be active in the outer court, helping the people, preaching the Gospel. This is what we will do, but God does not want us to live there. God does not want us to live in the holy place. There, as priests, we will serve God, testify of Him, worship Him, pray to Him; but this is not the place where we live. God wants us to dwell, to make our home, to live constantly and continuously in His presence, because our life is hid with Christ in God. God is now our home. There we shall abide. There we shall gaze upon Him. We shall see the glory of the Lord and be transformed from glory to glory according to His image, by the Lord, the Spirit.

So, how can we go through this time of great shaking and not be shaken off but be able to stand before God, holy and without blemish? The secret is that we must dwell within the veil. We must live day by day, hour by hour, moment by moment in the very presence of God, and this is something that our Lord Jesus has given to us. Again let us say, it is not for a privileged few. It is for every believer.

We would like to continue on with the second guidepost: "outside the camp." Within the veil and outside the camp—these are two related matters. In other words, if you live within the veil, then you will go outside the camp. To live within the veil is to live before God. To go outside the camp is to live before man. Within the veil speaks of our hidden life in God—unseen by man but seen by God. Outside the camp is our life before the world as a witness and a testimony for God. The more we live within the veil, the more we will go out of the spirit of the camp. The more we go out to Him, outside the camp, the more we will experience the closeness and the nearness of Him within the veil. These two things go together. Within the veil gives us the strength to go outside the camp and to go outside the camp confirms that which we have seen and heard within the veil. So, it is not enough that we live within the veil; but if we do, then we must go forth to Him outside the camp.

WHAT IS THE CAMP?

First of all, what is the camp? If you read Hebrews 13, you will find the phrases "outside the camp" and "outside the gate" are spoken of as if the camp and the city are one and the same thing. Now in a sense that is true. If you know the background, you know that after the children of Israel were delivered out of Egypt, as they were traveling through the wilderness, they were as a camp, the camp of God. Because they were traveling, therefore they camped along the way. But after they arrived in the promised land, then they dwelt in cities, and of course, the most well-known city was Jerusalem. So, as a matter of fact, the camp and the city are one and the same thing. It just shows that in the wilderness they camped, and in the promised land they dwelt in the city.

What is the meaning of a camp or a city? A camp or a city speaks to us of a certain boundary which is well organized into a unit. It is not scattered sands, but it is something that has been highly organized into a unit. There is a certain boundary there and that is what a camp or a city speaks of to us. Generally speaking, the world today is a camp or a city.

In the beginning, God created the earth and God gave the earth to man to live in, to enjoy, and to rule for Him; but unfortunately, man sinned against God. Through the fall of man, not only did man fall under the rule of the archenemy of God and man, Satan, but through man, Satan was able to usurp the earth. He took the earth from the hand of man and organized it into a cosmos, a system; so, the whole world today is a system. Whether it is political, or economic, or educational, or even religious, the whole world today is a system, a world system, organized by Satan as a unit. He uses this world system to oppose God, to fight against God's purpose, to try to delay the coming of the Kingdom of God. This is what the world is. It is a camp, a city, represented by Babylon.

Once we belonged to the world, we were part of it, we were under the dominion of the wicked one. But thank God, He has delivered us; He has taken us out of the world and has given us to His Son, our Lord Jesus. So what is our position today? We are in the world, but we are not of the world.

Now, it is not the will of God that we should go out of the world today. I often think how good it would be if the moment you are saved, you are raptured. That would save so many problems, but this is not God's will. Even though He has saved us, He has taken us out of the world and given us to Christ, and yet we are still in the world, physically speaking. But thank God, spiritually speaking, we are not of the world; in the world, but not of the world. It is the same as it was with our Lord Jesus. When He was on earth, He was in the world, but He was not of the world. This is our position. We do not belong to this world system, even though we are still here. Because of this we are exhorted not to love the world. "Love not the world, nor the things in the world. If any one loves the world. the love of the Father is not in him" (I John 2:15).

WHAT IS THE WORLD?

What is the world? The world is presented to us in the form of things. The world has many things, beautiful things, attractive things; and the world offers these things to entice, to draw out from us the lust of the flesh, the lust of the eyes, and the pride of life.

God created this earth for man to enjoy and God created us with desires and needs. These desires and needs will be met by the things that He created upon the earth. There is nothing wrong with these desires or needs that He has created in man. There is nothing wrong with the things that He created upon this earth to supply the needs of man; but today you find the enemy has organized the world and taken the things of the world to try to draw out the lusts from man.

What is lust? Lust is illegitimate desire. There is nothing wrong with desire. If you are hungry, you need to eat—nothing wrong with that; but, when the desire is drawn out to be inordinate, improper, illegitimate, out of bounds, then it becomes a lust. The enemy uses the things of the world to draw out the lust of the flesh. We not only want to live, but we want to live luxuriously. We want to satisfy our sinful passions. Our eyes are never satisfied with the things that we see. We want to compare ourselves with our neighbors—the pride of life. These are the things of the world and if we fall into the trap, then we will pierce ourselves with many sorrows and the love of the Father will not be in us.

The Bible exhorts us not to be conformed to the world. "Be not conformed to this world, but be transformed by the renewing of your mind, that ye may prove what is the good and acceptable and perfect will of God" (Romans 12:2).

In the original, *be not conformed to this world* means that the world is like a mold. Do not try to squeeze yourself into that mold. To put it in more modern language, do not try to be fashionable. You know, the world has a kind of mold, a kind of fashion. Every spring or every winter, you find the wind of fashion blows. Probably it starts in Paris or in New York, I don't know; and then when that fashion begins to blow, it blows all over the world. Everybody wants to follow the fashion—to squeeze themselves into that mold.

Dear brothers and sisters, you are too big for that mold; you are too dignified for that mold. You are not to follow the world; the world is to follow you. Why should we squeeze ourselves into the mold of the world, try to be fashionable? Now I do not mean that we should be so outdated as to be ancient, antique; we should be moderate. We should not try to be fashionable and squeeze ourselves into the mold of the world. The Bible tells us if we try to be friends with the world, the friendship of the world will make us enemies of God (see James 4:4).

We should not try to cultivate such friendship with the world as to compromise ourselves; because if we do, we become enemies of God. Go out of the camp. God has already delivered us out of this world. We do not belong. Do not try to go back and belong. If we do, we lose our testimony.

The Religious World

If you read the context of Hebrews, you will find this is not what the Holy Spirit is trying to define to us as what the camp is; it is not the world as such. It is as if, to the believers, the world, as a cosmos, should already be settled with us. We are not of the world—that's it. So, the writer of the Hebrews, or the Holy Spirit, is not so much concerned with the world as a camp or a city. The burden of the writer concerning this camp or city which we need to come forth from is not the world as such; rather it is the religious world.

Let me read to you a comment by Andrew Murray:

The camp was not Rome with its heathenism but Jerusalem with its religion and its revelation from God. There, Jesus was rejected of the Jews because He condemned their self-righteousness and formality. It is not the irreligious but the religious world from which we must go out; that is, from everything that is not in harmony with His cross and its spirit of self-sacrifice. Let us go forth; not from one religious connection to another, which in time proves to have as much of the spirit of the camp. No, let us go forth unto Him to closer fellowship, to more entire conformity to Him, the crossbearer, to His meek and patient and loving Spirit. Let us not cast our reproach on those we leave behind, but let us bear His reproach.

Another comment, this time by Robert Govett:

How does this apply to us now? Many interpret as those believers of any intelligence were justified in holding no fellowship with those assemblies of believers who have not as much light as themselves. This is certainly not the mind of Christ. It is good to leave idolatry such as that of Rome and every worldly system calling itself Christian which is really only an association of unbelievers with which some believers are mixed up.

Another comment by G.H. Lang:

The temple is the center of earthly, ritualistic, legalistic religion. This religion is in the city. It is the religion of the world, part of its system, but God is not in the city or its temple. When in Christ He came to it (that is God came to it) He was cast out into the place of curse. All classes of the city combined to despise and reject Him, the religious leaders, priests and rabbis, the politicians and the men of law, judges, police officers, learned scribes and the common people. All joined in thrusting Him away. Neither the city nor the temple saw Him again. He is not there and it is vain to seek Him there. It is at Calvary He must be first met and Calvary, the place of reproach, the only drawing unto the kingdom, the house, the heart, the glory of God. In plain language, it means that he who wishes to have fellowship with God in His holy heaven must abandon every system of religion that is of law, of ceremonies, of self-effort, of human devising, of secular authority, and must accept the reproach of dependence upon a fresh fellowship with, of obedience to the redeemer who suffered without the gate.

The camp was Judaism at the time of Christ and at the time of the first century before the destruction of the temple. Judaism had its beginning, its origin from God. God gave to Moses the law, the priesthood, the sacrifices. It had its beginning in God, but gradually through the hands of man it had become an "ism," an organized system. Instead of a revelation from above, it had become a tradition of men.

CHRIST WAS CAST OUTSIDE THE CAMP

So at the time of Christ, Judaism was a religious system. At the top of the system was the high priest and with him were the seventy members of the Sanhedrin, the governing body of Judaism. Then there were the Sadducees, the Pharisees, the scribes, the rabbis. Judaism was highly organized at the time of Christ. The high priest, the Sanhedrin, the Pharisees, the scribes—these were the governing body of Judaism. They defined and explained everything in Judaism; they were the authority. They controlled not only the body but the conscience of the Jewish people. If anyone dared to contradict their interpretations and concepts, they were excommunicated, cast out of the commonwealth of Israel. When Christ, the Messiah came, they cast Him out, because Christ did not fit in with their interpretation of prophecy or with their concept of the Messiah. They expected a political Messiah, a Messiah that would come and deliver them out of the iron hand of Rome and make them the head of the nations. Instead, this Jesus of Nazareth came and preached about love and forgiveness. He had no interest in overthrowing the Roman yoke, but He was interested in delivering people from the yoke of sin. He did not fit in with their concept; He did not fit in with their interpretation. He did not follow them; He did not belong to the system. He dared to challenge their system and their tradition; and because of this, they got rid of Him: "Away with Him, away with Him, crucify Him" (see John 19:15).

There was no place for the Messiah. It was a camp and Christ was cast outside of the camp. They brought Him outside of Jerusalem to the place called Golgotha, the place of skull, and there they crucified Him with two robbers. They did not know that it was a fulfillment of prophecy.

It was a fulfillment of type because in the Old Testament, in Leviticus 16, you find the Day of Atonement, that great Day of Atonement. Now it is true the sacrifices were offered on the altar daily, day after day—sin offering, trespass offering. But on the Day of Atonement, a bullock and a goat were offered and the blood of the goat and the bullock was carried by the high priest behind the veil and sprinkled upon the mercy seat. There, the high priest made atonement for himself and for the people once a year before God. All the sacrifices, sin offerings that were offered day after day were for personal reasons, but on the Day of Atonement that sacrifice was offered for the atonement of the whole nation. The blood was brought behind the veil to the very presence of God to make atonement for the high priest and for the people. But the bodies of the sacrifice were not to be eaten by the priests or those who offered, like the peace offerings. They were not to be burned on the altar completely like the burnt offering. No. The bodies of the goat and the bullock were carried outside the camp and there they were burned into ashes. The body was burned outside the camp; the blood was brought within the veil.

Here you will find how it was fulfilled in the life of our Lord Jesus. How they pushed Him out of the temple, out of the city to that place outside the camp, a place of curse, of reproach! There they crucified Him. His body was broken at Calvary, but thank God, the blood was brought behind the veil to atone for the sins of the world. In order to sanctify the people, He was crucified outside the gate.

Why must the bullock and goat have been burned outside the camp while the blood was brought within the veil? Because the camp was unclean, was defiled. In Exodus chapter 32, when Moses was at the top of the mountain receiving the ten commandments, the children of Israel were below in the plain worshipping the golden calf. God sent Moses down and when Moses saw the scene, he broke the two tablets of stone, the law, because they had broken the law. He ground the golden calf into powder, cast it upon the water, and ordered the children of Israel to drink of the water, that is, to drink of their own sin.

Then you remember how Moses stood at the gate of the camp and said, "Whoever is with the Lord, come to me." Only the tribe of Levi came out of the camp to join with Moses. Moses ordered them to go into the camp from one gate to the other and slay everyone they met, whether men, women or children, their relatives or their neighbors, to sanctify themselves.

Then in Exodus 33, something happened. Moses took his own tent, removed it from the camp, pitched it outside the camp and called it the tent of meeting. Whenever people wanted to inquire of God they went outside of the camp to the tent of meeting. When Moses went out of the camp to the tent, the glory of the Lord, the pillar of fire descended upon it. The people saw it and they worshipped. The camp was so defiled that Moses had to remove his tent outside the camp and God's glory came upon that tent.

Christ, in order to sanctify us, could not do this work within the camp. Judaism was supposed to prepare for the coming of the

Messiah, and yet He was not received; it was defiled. So He had to do the work of redemption outside the gate. There—outside the camp—He was crucified in order to bring His blood into heaven, into the very presence of God to atone for the sins of the world.

LET US GO FORTH TO HIM

That is the reason the Bible says, "Let us go forth to Him outside the camp." He is not in the camp, He is outside; therefore, anyone who wants to seek Him has to go outside the camp to seek Him.

If you read Acts 7, in the testimony that Stephen gave, he told the people the same thing. Jerusalem, the temple—God is no longer there. You have to go out to meet the Lord. But Judaism, as a camp, had not only rejected Christ, they persecuted those who followed Christ.

How does it apply to us today? Christianity has its origin from heaven. It began as a living revelation. It is a living faith. It is like a mustard seed. The Lord said, "If your faith is like a mustard seed . . .". The mustard seed is the smallest of all seeds, but there is life there. This faith comes from above. When Peter acknowledged our Lord Jesus as the Christ, the Son of the living God, Christ said, "Peter, son of Jonah, you are blessed because this is revealed to you by My Father who is in heaven." It is a living faith.

After the death, resurrection, and ascension of Christ, at the day of Pentecost the Church had its beginning. Within thirty years the Gospel was preached to the world that was known at that time, because in the 28th chapter of Acts, Paul was in Rome, the end of the world, the center of the world. In thirty years the Gospel was preached throughout the world that was known at that time. The Roman Empire used its military and political power to try to wipe out Christ, Christianity, but the Roman Empire was wiped out. Christ and His followers conquered not by the sword, but by love.

As this mustard seed grows, and it should grow, it should be a vegetable because this is the will God. The church of God should remain in this world small, despised in the eyes of men.

But unfortunately, starting before the fourth century, man's hand began to come in to organize the living faith, to organize the revelation from above. Gradually they have reduced it into an organization, an institution, powerful in this world. It has become a tradition instead of revelation, a system instead of living faith. This mustard seed has grown abnormally into a big tree out of its kind, out of God's order and all the birds of the air have come and roosted upon it. If you read the first parable in Matthew 13, you know the birds represent the wicked ones. Instead of becoming the habitation of the Holy God, it has become the roosting place of all wickedness.

In the beginning, Christianity was like three measures of meal to be offered to God as an oblation, a meal offering. But then you find the woman came and put leaven in it. Leaven in the Scripture speaks of wicked doctrines or wicked manners. The leaven blew up the three measures of meal, making it palatable to human taste but unfit to be offered to God. This is what Christianity has become. Just like Judaism, it had its beginning in heaven, in God, but now it has become an earthly, human, religious system. What happened to this system? They pushed Christ out of the camp.

If you read church history, you will find during the first three centuries, the world, as a cosmos, as a system, opposed Christ and persecuted His followers. The Roman Empire persecuted the Christians. If you want to read how Christians died read *Foxe's Book of Martyrs.* There you will find how people like Polycarp and others gave their lives for Christ and how the Roman Empire tried to wipe out Christianity— burning them, casting them to the lions, killing them. But the blood of the martyrs became the seed of the Gospel and the Gospel spread. After the fourth century, Christianity became a religious system, part of the world. After it became a religious system, part of the world, what happened? It began to persecute those who wanted to follow the Lamb whithersoever He goes. It is no surprise for the world to persecute Christians; but for the religious, Christian world to persecute Christians, is surprising—but it is a fact.

I would like to read to you what Andrew Murray said:

There is perhaps no greater need in our day than that God should open the eye of His people to the solemn truth that the so-called Christian world is the very same world that rejected Christ. We are to bear to it the same relation he did.

Strong words, but true words.

When you come to the sixth century, the Roman Catholic system was firmly established. Do you want to know how the Roman Catholic system persecuted the true believers of Christ? Let me read you some—just a little bit. If you want to read, there are volumes and volumes of it.

The Paulicians

In the middle of the seventh century, the Paulicians existed in the area of Mesopotamia. We do not know why they are called Paulicians, probably because they put much emphasis on the writings of Paul. They had a particular respect for the authority of the Bible, advocated a life of simplicity, were a devout and earnest people, and bore a strong witness against the unsavory practice of the Catholic Church. Their enemies testified against them, but their lives testified of Christ.. The Paulicians accepted no central authority to rule over the scattered assemblies. The local churches looked to God as their Head, and they were built up and strengthened spiritually by teachers who moved from place to place to minister in their midst. Their spiritual unity lay in the life which they had in Christ. They were the people who wanted to follow the Lamb whithersoever He goes.

But do you know what happened? Their leaders were killed and in the middle of the ninth century there was notorious persecution under Empress Theodora. Within the space of five years a hundred thousand persons met their death. The Catholic system used the world to kill these followers of Jesus because they did not belong to the camp.

The Bogomils

In the middle of the eighth century, the Bogomils, which simply means "friends of God," lived in the Balkan Peninsula. They preached love and grace from the Gospels and exhibited the Christian virtues in their lives. Instead of ornate church buildings with all the attendant trappings, meeting places were plain and void of bells, images and altars, or the believers could meet equally well within their own homes. The Scriptural truth of the priesthood of all believers was recognized; the congregations were governed by a plurality of elders and edified through the teaching of ministering brothers. The poor and needy among the churches were also helped according to the law of love in Christ.

The spread of these Friends of God constituted an increasing threat to the Roman Church and Rome was not inactive in seeking to stem the tide of this meek and powerful opposition. The king of Hungary was ordered to invade Bosnia and the country was ravaged by war that went on for years.

The Cathars

Another illustration is in the 12th and 13th centuries. The Cathars, also known as the Albigenses, fearlessly denounced the prevalent ecclesiastical errors of the day and led people to a new life through the preaching of the Scriptures.

The Waldeneses

The Waldeneses were characterized by their marked reverence for the Scriptures in which they found their rule of daily living and church rule. The knowledge of Christ's dwelling within by the Spirit was to them the truth of paramount importance; but in the matter of Scripture interpretation which did not deny the basic necessity of this experience of Christ, they allowed a generous liberty. Salvation was through faith, and the Roman Church had authority neither to open nor to close the door to God's grace. The proof of salvation was holiness of life. Baptism was a testimony to faith in Christ, and the Lord's supper was a remembrance of His sacrifice.

But then in 1348, under Charles IV, Emperor of the Holy Roman Empire, a determined effort was at once instituted to stamp out the Christian congregations. An Inquisition was brought into effect with diabolical efficiency. How that religious system, called Christian, persecuted those who belonged to Christ, who wanted to follow Christ all the way, because they did not belong to the camp!

The Reformation

But do you think this only happened with the Roman Catholic system? No. Thank God for the Reformation in the 16th century. Thank God for Luther, Calvin, Zwingli, and these people through whom God has recovered justification by faith and the open Bible. Unfortunately, these reformers did not go far enough. In other words, they came short of God and even though they came out of the Roman yoke, they came under the different states or countries—national religion, national church.

In the beginning, it was a move of God, but then man came in and organized it and they became state churches. Protestantism is no better than Catholicism. If you read church history, at the time of the Reformation, even the reformers themselves, who were persecuted by the Roman Catholic system, in turn persecuted those who wanted to follow the Lord all the way.

We know more about these things today than before because through research many hidden histories have been recovered.

The Anabaptists

The Anabaptists are an illustration. Actually, *Anabaptist* is a very general, vague term. It does not actually refer to any particular group, but it simply means those who are baptized again. Why? Because you find during the time of Reformation even people like Martin Luther still believed in infant baptism. But there were some people who were not involved in Catholicism or Protestantism. They were freed from the bondage of either and they were able to go into the Word of God in such simplicity that they began to see that baptism is believer's baptism. In other words, they could not find infant baptism in the Word of God, but they had all been baptized in the Roman system or in Protestant churches as infants. So when they began to follow the Lord and be baptized by water, they were called Anabaptists, those who baptize again; but actually, they were baptized for the first time.

These people refused to call themselves by any other name but Christian or brother. They admitted baptism only to those who had had an experience of regeneration through faith in Christ; but how they were persecuted. Even by the reformers, they were killed, burned— hundreds, hundreds—drowned. They said, "All right. You want to be baptized; we will baptize you." Then they tied a rock around their neck and drowned them—men, women and children, hundreds and hundreds of them.

This happened not only at the time of Reformation, but if you read on in church history, even in England there was persecution. People who dissented, people who refused to take the oath of loyalty to the king (because the king was supposed to be the head of the church) were dissenters, non-conformists, and how they were persecuted. John Bunyan wrote *The Pilgrim's Progress* in prison. He was in prison twelve years.

Thank God, in the 18th century, there was Zinzendorf. He opened his estate to receive those Moravians who were persecuted by the religious Christian world because of their faith. That was the beginning of the Moravian mission.

Think of John Wesley and George Whitefield. God used them, but they were not allowed to preach in so-called churches. So finally, they preached in the church graveyard.

This has continued on and on and on up to our time. How those true believers of Christ in China were persecuted, more by the so-called Christian world than the secular world. It is true the Communist government persecuted them, but it is that organization, so-called Christian organization, used by the Communists that did the persecution.

There is no place for Christ in the camp. He is not there and that is why the Word says, "Therefore let us go forth to Him without the camp." If you want to follow the Lord, you have to go forth outside the camp to Him.

We need to live within the veil, but at the same time we have to go outside the camp. Why? What do you have outside the camp? If you read the Old Testament you find that:

People who are cast outside the camp are the lepers—Leviticus 13.

People who are cast outside the camp to be killed are the blasphemers—Leviticus 24.

People who are cast outside the camp are the Sabbath breakers—Numbers 15.

It is a place of curse and reproach and that is the place where they cast our Christ. Therefore, let us go forth to Him. The only attraction outside the camp is HIM, because He is there. Where He is, there we need to be, bearing His reproach.

LIFE OUTSIDE THE CAMP

Now, what is the kind of life outside the camp? First of all, it is A LIFE OF SEPARATION. We need to be separated. We need to be separated from the world as a system, even if it is religious, because only through such separation are we able to join completely with the Lord.

Separation and unity are not contradictory. Separation is unto unity—you find that in John

17. The Lord said, "You are not of the world. I sanctify myself that they may be sanctified." Why? "That they may be one as I and the Father are one." Today, if we are not separated from the world, we will not be able to be united into one. It is a life of separation.

It is A LIFE OF REPROACH. It is the way of the cross. We have to bear His reproach. We have to take up the cross and follow Him. We will be misunderstood; we will be labeled; we will be accused; but this is where He is.

It is A LIFE OF FAITH because we do not have an abiding city here. We are looking for that city with foundation. We acknowledge ourselves as strangers, as sojourners upon this earth. We do not expect anything on this earth; our expectation is in Him. It is a life of faith. We do not walk by sight, but by faith.

Thank God, it is A LIFE OF WORSHIP. Why? Because it is said, "By Him, therefore let us offer the sacrifice of praise continually to God" (see Hebrews 13:15). Now you would think that people in the camp, with everything, living such a comfortable, unchallenged life, welcome by everybody, would certainly be able to offer praises unto God. But strange to say, it is those who are outside the camp who are able to offer the sacrifice of praise by Christ Jesus.

What is the sacrifice of praise? A sacrifice costs you something; it hurts you in a sense; you need to sacrifice something. How many praises unto God are but lip service? There is no sacrifice involved. It is easy just to open your mouth and praise the Lord. It does not cost you anything. This is not the sacrifice of praise. The sacrifice of praise costs you something because you follow the Lamb whithersoever He goes, because you bear His reproach. It costs you something and out of the sacrifice, praises ascend to Him. That is the sacrifice of praise and that kind of praise satisfies God's heart. Those who are outside the camp live a life of worship.

"Of doing good and communicating of your substance do not forget, for with such sacrifices God is well pleased." Do you think it is those who live in prosperity and comfort and popularity that give? No. Those who give are those who suffer.

The Macedonian believers, oh, how they gave! They gave, not out of their bounty, but out of their lack. Because they loved God so much, they gave themselves to God and they wanted to have a part in the grace of giving. But the Corinthians—you have to collect from them.

Those who are outside the camp are those who take care of the poor, think of the needy, are willing to sacrifice themselves in order to satisfy, to supply other people. This is the life we are expected to live.

In this day of great shaking, if we live within the veil and we go forth outside the camp, we will be kept by the Lord through the great shaking and be able to stand before His presence, holy and without blemish.

Shall we pray:

Our heavenly Father, we do thank Thee for giving us instructions, telling us how we should live in this time of great shaking. Our Father, we do pray that by the work of the Holy Spirit, we may be a people who live within the veil in heaven and go outside the camp here below. We ask Thee,

O Lord, that these may be the characteristics of our life on earth, to the glory of Thy name. We ask in the name of our Lord Jesus. Amen.

Other Books Printed By
Christian Testimony Ministry

WHY DO WE SO GATHER?
WORSHIP

LANCE LAMBERT   CALLED UNTO HIS ETERNAL GLORY
GOD'S ETERNAL PURPOSE
IN THE DAY OF THY POWER
JACOB I HAVE LOVED
LIVING FAITH
LESSONS FROM THE LIFE OF MOSES
LOVE DIVINE
MY HOUSE SHALL BE A HOUSE OF PRAYER
PREPARATION FOR THE COMING OF THE LORD
REIGNING WITH CHRIST
SPIRITUAL CHARACTER
THE GOSPEL OF THE KINGDOM
THE IMPORTANCE OF COVERING
THE LAST DAYS AND GOD'S PRIORITIES
THE PRIZE
THE SUPREMACY OF JESUS CHRIST
THINE IS THE POWER!
THOU ART MINE

T. AUSTIN-SPARKS   THE LORD'S TESTIMONY AND THE WORLD NEED

HARVEY CEDARS CONFERENCE

STEPHEN KAUNG   HEAVENLY VISION
SPIRITUAL RESPONSIBILITY

CONGDON, HILE, KAUNG   SPIRITUAL MINISTRY
SPIRITUAL AUTHORITY
SPIRITUAL HOUSE
SPIRITUAL SUBMISSION

STEPHEN KAUNG   SPIRITUAL KNOWLEDGE
SPIRITUAL POWER
SPIRITUAL REALITY
SPIRITUAL VALUE
SPIRITUAL BLESSING
SPIRITUAL DISCERNMENT

Spiritual Warfare
Spiritual Ascendancy
Spiritual Mindedness
Spiritual Perfection
Spiritual Fulness
Spiritual Sonship
Spiritual Stewardship
Spiritual Travail
Spiritual Inheritance
Harvey Cedars Conference:
Hile, Kaung, Lambert
The King is Coming

9 781942 521518